For David,

some homegrown leaves
for quiet enjoyment,

all good things,

Symon

October 2003

CINQUEFOIL

CINQUEFOIL

New work from five Ottawa poets

Mark Frutkin
Rebecca Leaver
Seymour Mayne
Susan Robertson
Nicola Vulpe

mosaic press

National Library of Canada Cataloguing in Publication

Cinquefoil : new work from five Ottawa poets / Mark
Frutkin ... [et al.].

ISBN 0-88962-811-4

1. Canadian poetry (English)--Ontario--Ottawa. 2. Canadian poetry
(English)--21st century. I. Frutkin, Mark, 1948-

PS8295.7.O8C55 2003   C811'.5408'0971384   C2003-905410-1

Published by Mosaic Press, offices and warehouses at 1252 Speers Road,
Units 1 & 2, Oakville, Ontario L6L 5N9, Canada and Mosaic Press,
PMB 145, 4500 Witmer Industrial Estates, Niagara Falls, NY 14305-
1386, USA.

Mosaic Press acknowledges the assistance of the Canada Council and
the Department of Canadian Heritage, Government of Canada for
their support of our publishing programme.

THE CANADA COUNCIL | LE CONSEIL DES ARTS
FOR THE ARTS | DU CANADA

Mosaic Press in Canada:
1252 Speers Road, Units 1 & 2,
Oakville, Ontario
L6L 5N9
Phone/Fax: 905-825-2130
mosaicpress@on.aibn.com

Mosaic Press in the USA:
4500 Witmer Industrial Estates,
PMB 145, Niagara Falls, NY
14305-1386
Phone/Fax: 1-800-387-8992
mosaicpress@on.aibn.com

www.mosaic-press.com

Contents

"Why these poets together?" always seems to be asked of collections like *Cinquefoil*, that is, collections of poetry by several authors not proposing to launch a new school, or a new ism or anti-ism. Or at least that is what the prefaces to these sorts of collections seem to assume and attempt to answer. *Cinquefoil* is no different.

Winters in Ottawa are long and dark. In the long, dark winter of 1997 several of us got together at a local watering hole to talk poetry. Then we did it again. And again.

Our group evolved from gathering to gathering; at times we were as many as twenty, often fewer. There were poets with national and international reputations, and poets known mostly to their friends.

Six years later, we're still minding our thirst, talking poetry, writing the stuff – and still speaking to each other, which if you've frequented poets you'll recognize as no small feat in itself. So it's time to share.

And, yes, the reason, the unifying principle: we all live in Ottawa, the east side of Ottawa to be precise, though this fact has no bearing on the discussion; but also and more to the point: all of us believe that poetry is about something more than itself, and we're unrepentant lovers of the word. It is this belief and this love that unites us, nothing more – but nothing less.

MARK FRUTKIN

SEVENTEEN THINGS DIFFICULT TO ACCOMPLISH

*A poem inspired by the first book of poetry – Guide to Capturing
a Plum Blossom by Sung Po-jen*

Capture a plum blossom in high wind.
Carry the ant's load.
Hold the butterfly this side of the fence.
Keep pace with the arrow.
Know when the leaf will let go.
Separate the sea from the tears of fish.
Grow younger and younger.
Keep the bee from its flower.
Count emptiness.
Split the wind in two.
Stop the moon from shrinking.
Prolong a night of love.
Read the cloud entirely from beginning to end.
Retrace your steps in the river.
Picture your own face without a mirror.
Lose yourself completely in the mountain.

A Walk in the Gatineau Hills with Basho

Come with me, old one,
on this last journey,
on this first warm day
of spring, before the black flies
and mosquitoes reclaim their forest.

The air crisscrossed with scents
of blossoming trees,
your old mind still clear
as a calm pool
reflecting the world –
we can walk for hours
and say nothing at all.
We've left the city behind,
a place too busy
to feel its own sadness.

In high places we gaze out,
in low places we look down
at mosses and grasses and new life.
We hear the whisper of brooks,
the piercing lonely cry of birds.

I turn around and you are gone –
all that's left is this
walking stick of oak
bent like your spine.

Koan Poem

I dreamt that I was not dreaming.
I sang out, quite tunefully, that I could not sing.
I thought that I was not thinking,
was running because I knew I could not run,
and once in love
realized I was not in love.
I only wrote down the invisible words,
said what was unspeakable,
while dreaming, did not dream.

MOUNTAIN CALLIGRAPHY

The blank page has an inconceivable longing
for the touch of the brush.

The brush longs to soak
in thick rich ink.

The ink has an unquenchable desire to flow
down the mountain's face.

A thousand years ago.
A thousand years from now.
This same clear wind.

Little grasshopper,
You've let go of your carapace,
Nothing inside.

The last day of July –
Who would expect an outflowing of poetry
At such a late date?

Even though they foolishly cut down
The old pine along the road,
Never forget.

Every summer the maple tree grows another foot,
But it's so huge
No one notices.

"Andromeda flowers",
the stars fade
with the light of dawn.

Another year gone by,
Another moment –
Cicadas.

The kite snaps its string
And disappears –
a hawk arrives.

An Old Copy of the Heart Sutra

I have a copy of the Heart Sutra,
a single sheet
of the Buddha's teaching on emptiness.
The paper is old, yellowing, fading away,
beginning to crumble at the edges.
I picture it slowly disappearing
as I hold it in my hands,
as it ages and dissolves,
as its fibers decay
and fall into fragments,
drifting down between my fingers,
leaving me holding nothing
but light in my hands.

Cathedral of Chartres, Built in Silence

Thirty-thousand labourers as if in communal prayer
offered in silence – oh, there were sounds:
of masons tapping stone, of carts creaking,
of men and women grunting under loaded hods,
but even the birds noticed and ceased their singing.

Once a workman sneezed and everyone looked up –
what a strange and marvelous noise it was.
And, of course, the consumptives
could not help but cough
though they tried to do their part.
The architect walked about with a board
and a piece of charcoal
and was quick to sketch what before was spoken.
They could hear thunder across the plain miles away,
and the sound of a nearby brook
unable to curb its babbling.

NEW YEAR COME AND GONE

Another New Year come and gone,
feeding my days into the empty mouth of time,
crumbling off chunks of myself,
like a cliff chocking into the sea.
Years ago when I was a child
I never thought this day would come,
each day passes, a cloud unfolding,
somersaulting across the sky,
chasing the sun and finding the moon,
full now, but shrinking away in my hands.

Music

Frigid morning,
smoke from chimneys
drifts past three hydro wires
like musical notation,
multi-stringed trees
accompanied by light
moved by wind,
white hum of the refrigerator
and the vast drone of snow –
all is music:
traffic, furnace blow,
voice and radio,
all sings,
all sings.

OLD FRIEND
for Jochen

My old friend, we are aging
at exactly the same rate,
hair going grey and thin,
our young sons laughing at us
as if they themselves will never grow old.
How many more warm summer nights will we see?
The silence of the void begins
to penetrate us even as we go out to meet it.
We share a few quiet beers and looking
at each other, see ourselves.

The News

1.) One Year After 9/11

My TV is an eye,
one that fills up with tears
a drop at a time.
My TV is weeping
like one of those strange statues
of the Virgin Mary,
weeping until it leaks onto the floor.

2.) Weight

The weight of news drives me deep into the couch,
having misspent a Saturday morning
reading the paper,
anvil of words sinks to the bottom of my brain pan.
Shall I scurry back to bed
and hide under the sheets?
The world is too much written,
everyone has an opinion
and a little book to sell
in three volumes.

Freeing the Poem

Using a broken axe handle,
its voluptuous curve
like his woman's hip,
a man tries to move a stone
that embraces the earth, rooted
in silence.

As he works, grunts rumble
from deep in his chest.

At last the stone rolls
once over,
releasing on the air,
a puzzled butterfly.

KING IN EXILE
for Jeffrey Street

The exiled king paces gingerly
in his linoleum kitchen
from orange juice to toast to coffee.
Every other thought he thinks is this:
When will the call come,
the letter posted through the door?
And between those thoughts he thinks:
It will never come.
I am breakfasting between hope and despair.

The kitchen is draughty, silent.
The long stairs leading down beckon,
his throne there, at the end of time,
waiting.

Heavy industry came from the Romans,
bridges and roads too.
Politics, philosophy and pure mathematics
were a gift of the Greeks.
We can thank the Egyptians for mysticism
while the alphabet, farming and religion
came from the Middle East.
Our bones are from Africa
and the roots of language itself
are found in India.
The Jews gave us banking, trade and commerce,
humour and complaint,
and the Chinese discovered
gunpowder, paper money and rice.
The Japanese offered an elegant aesthetic
and the shortest poems on record.
Siberia gave us our concept
of cold and distant exile,
while Canada gave us snow and clean blue space.
We can thank France for individual freedoms,
cooking as high art
and the idea of the avant garde.
The Scotch gave us single malt.
The English gave us the stiff upper lip
and the gin and tonic (with lemon or lime)
while the Irish gave us the music of words.
The Americans gave us baseball
while music came from the slaves
(except for the odd balalaika and the accordion).

The Spanish contributed a love of gold
and cruelty and flirting with death,
while the Italians gave us a love of light
and a clear sense of romance.
The Scandinavians provided blonde beauty
and the idea of official generosity.
From Germany we got mechanized horror,
brilliant physics, transcendent music and beer.
The Tibetans offered us the highest mountains
and a pure sense of loneliness,
while the Australians contributed
the modern-day traveler.
The Russians, meanwhile, showed us patience
in the face of grim futility,
and those dolls within dolls,
symbols of something important
though we're never quite sure what.
The coup came from South America
along with cocaine and beautiful skin.

REBECCA LEAVER

DEUS ABSCONDITUS

Only God may hide
His face.

The rest, masks flayed
live exposed in

The stippling of line
drawings

Impressed with narrowed
eyes, lifted brow

Naked, and not so beautiful
as Metatron.

Avian Composition

Could I play
The arpeggio of birds
Arrayed against the sky,

Ascending
       In perfect synchrony
       As if one brain
       Composed the score?

Would my hand stretch
       To span
              The full
                     Octave?

HIGH SUMMER

Long gone the stained sheet
Of virgin spring –

Rubenesque roses now

    Luscious *en deshabille*

        Lean seductively in doorways,

Brambles bolster a glut
        Of berries

Bees stagger

    Pollen-dazed

      Drowsy with heat

And musky post-coital scent.

IT IS ONLY

It is only 8:30

    A.M.

And already
Slouched on the park bench

You have uncorked the genie
With the right angle of your elbow.

Oblivious

To the clean crisp sheet of sky
That is tucked around the day,

The green smell of wind,
Asters dying in their beds,
The stiletto of loss.

DEVIL'S EGG

Pick up
The plain brown rock

About the size
Of a beating heart.

Feel the grainy heft
In your upturned palm.

Split it open:

Know how Adam felt
When light
Opened his eyes.

Pheasant Under Glass

His body ricochets
Off the hood

Arcs 180 degrees

Every feather
And pinion etched in bas relief

Lands on the roadside
Stuffed and dressed,

An entrée
At a Medieval banquet.

WINDFALL

If you bit her

      she'd be soft,

over-ripe and bruised.

Plagued by wasps

drawn by the sweet, sticky juice –

An apple picked

      warily

from the orchard floor.

In Times of Chaos

Wield an iron

Over vast expanses
Of damp, wrinkled sheets.

Never mind that
Objects, in defiance

Of gravity,
Fly around the room.

Inhale

Thoughts like steam,
Pressed and crisp

Faintly scented
With sunlight and bluing.

FROZEN CLOTHES

Neighbors find it odd
Of a January midnight
To catch her pegging clothes,

Yet moonlight does as well
When the purpose
Is to freeze
The wild scent of winter
And watch wind
Sculpt wet sheets

And socks
Into erections
Priapus would envy.

BREAKFAST OF CHAMPIONS

Refracted light spills
Into my cereal bowl,
Puddles in the milk.

With each spoonful
I get rainbows,
Not bananas,

With each spoonful
I am eating light
For breakfast.

WITH HILARY

I saw a rogue owl

   drift

Barred wings unfurled

Like the Angel Gabriel

Over a star-blind city.

Walked as a blind man
Stumbling on stones and roots

Felt heat rise in my palms

Until the moon rose,
A wafer
Dipped in blood.

SNOW SHOEING

Do you suppose
    This was the way Jesus felt
        Stepping onto the waves

When water alone
    Held the weight
        Of his body?

Unlike faithless Peter
    I place my shoes
        On fickle snow

Cross unknown drifts
    On graceless feet
        Amazed.

Looking at My Son's Arm

I am looking
at my son's arm
as he leans
on the dining room table,
grinning

A man's arm –
the only part
that is vulnerable,
(that and the smile)

He is otherwise
armoured,
a bullet-proof vest
covers his heart.

I am thinking
of the David:
the vein in his hand
is also pulsing
in my son's.

Seeing My Father for the Last Time

He has a tag attached
to the toe of his left foot

the kind you see
at clearance sales

his body covered
by a sheet

like shrouded furniture
in an abandoned house

a rocking chair unused
and chests unopened

in this grief-dwelling
what I feel
is absence of fear.

BETRAYAL

Being but three
She can stand upright
On the car seat
Next to her dad
(in the days before seat belts
 were *de rigueur*)
Her soft unruly hair
brushing the felt liner.

Wehavetodosomethingaboutthathair
Is a statement she doesn't understand,

Doesn't understand
Being left with strangers
And shorn
Like a boy.

Everything Moves Toward the Light

Skeletal fingers
Under the sink
Reach for the sliver,

Defying Darwin
The moth dives
Into the flame,

Seaweed stretches
For the mirrored surface
Of the lake,

The dark side
Of the moon
Chases the sun,

And even I
Keep moving
Toward the end of the tunnel.

Seymour Mayne

PRACTICE RUN

What is this sleep?
                      Practice?
I put up my feet
    to float into reverie.
I smile, cheeks
    burnished with joy,
like a nobleman joining
the Pharaoh on his hot
dry run
        into sand.

BEGINNING

As if taking a long deserved nap
the old sparrow lay quiet
by the front porch. Earlier in the evening
it had come, longing for rest,
warmed by the setting sun –
once more it opened its tiny eyes, blue
and sunken as if it were slowly flying
back through its own pupils
receding until it became a pulsing spot,
then just a distant dot,
at last simply still and invisible
as it once was
at the very, very beginning.

ABOVE THE PUERTA
for Bernd Dietz

Scattering
        above the Puerta
                de Almodóvar
loud
     formations
             of sparrows
rise
    over the palms,
              break into arcs,
wheel back again
          towards the gravity
                  of the tower.

Why
    should they
            guide themselves
to our feet
      or plentiful
            crumbs?
They are high,
         higher now
               than the pacific sun
which earlier
        nudged them into
              the thousand and one
perches and shelters
         by the gardens
            along the ancient walls.

Afire
    with flight
        they pepper
the air,
    careening buckshot
aimed
    at the ceramic blue.

They shatter the peace
    with yet
        another lunge
before night
    settles them into
        the armistice of sleep.

Córdoba
November 2000

CÓRDOBA

There is a smell of leather
        in Córdoba,
of tanned hide.

Even the walls
        and squares
are stricken
as if with the slow
strokes of a tanner.
They are thickened
        by each blow
of submission
without word, past
        glory preserved.

Hold Córdoba snugly
        under your arm,
hold her close
        full as she is,
a seasoned satchel
bleached and baked
by the impassive
        but crafty sun.

TEN

Of the first fright: one,
of shadows breaking away
    from words: two,
of wings fluttering in the night:
    three,
of books standing like angels on guard:
    four –

But of the knife, five and six,
and the bully with the revolver,
    seven, eight and nine,
and of the trigger-happy finger –
    ten
ready to do their part
    in staving off the plagues.

JONAH

How does one die?
Does it burst out like a flood
rising for a lifetime
to its level of escape?

Or does it coil
around in the cave of a dream,
shutting off the vista of light
with a sudden jerk

and the silence holds
louder than God?

DAUGHTERS OF PROPHECY

She who approaches
    meets sentinel of stone.

      *

Do not let his shield
    detract you.

He too was once frail
    flesh and bone.

      *

At the brush of eyelids
    return him to muscle and skin.

With a light touch
    he will recover speech.

      *

He proclaims in the square
    and challenges kin!

      *

You wait for the words to end,
    then quickly embrace.

He abandons his jeremiads,
    becomes dumb with joy.

Yet lingers to remain stone
    – but not his face.

       *

There his eyes sink
        close lidded
and he curls into
        dormant dreams.

       *

Hail, women
       Levites of Zion,
daughters of prophecy
       who encircle the hill –

       *

To the unfaithful,
       hard of heart,
Jerusalem will not yield
       even one of her gates!

REAL ESTATE

My father passed on
          no faithful piety.
Whomever he may
          have addressed in prayer
the name was never bequeathed
          in letter or will.

Nor did he let on who
          sent his guardian angel
to wave his way
          – when he was barely tall –
from the ripe horizon
          of a field of high grain.
Out there he was safe
          in sun or beating rain.

He never forgot
          those pear trees
hung with succulent gold
          and the maturing soil
yielding what was tastiest
          from his distant
corner of Ukraine.

Here in his last town,
          Montreal,
he held no plot dearer
          than his backyard,

his row of tomato plants
  and cucumbers inching
forward in green formation
  to a briny fate.

Who will tend
  with the same devotion
his final real
  estate in De la Savane,
claimed as it will be
  to the end
with his bare
  chiselled name?

BREADCRUMBS
in memory of Shoshi Hyman

Will the blue birds
          perch today
with breadcrumbs in their beaks
or with wings still
          rest in the back garden
where your abandoned studio stands
          behind the spacious house
on Ben Maimon?

You were always on a tight schedule,
          too too busy
– so what was the rush,
          Shoshi,
to leave so soon?

June 9, 1996
22 Sivan 5756

PEBBLES
for Ben Hollander

However hewn the stones of Jerusalem,
the fine pebbles of Camp Ramah
reveal a more modest finish.
Scraped smooth from the slow retreat
of crushing glaciers,
                              they have learned
the silence of long seasons
endlessly repeating under the impassive
Canadian sky.
                  They have less
to say, perhaps nothing at all:
blood trickling into their veins of ore
draws from expiring mosquitoes –
or from bloodroot
                        yielding its sanguine
essence without pain,
                              without the piercing
shrapnel of speech.

Skeleton Lake, Muskoka

WHOSE LIGHT
in memory of Louis Dudek

Whose light is this anyway?
A cosmic stunt
for credulous eyes?

While beyond the exponential
                distance
the darkness enfolds itself
up to the first second

before the crack
of instant creation –
Who believes in light
                everlasting

enlightening
silence, darkness
and the first and final word?

EQUINOX

If
early
light
returns,
is
there
renewed
hope
for
ailing
tongues
rising
in
darkness?

CROWS

The
crows
of
Sandy
Hill
are
much
too
big,
sleek
with
wide
bristling
wings.

HAIL

Hail peppered the air like seed
        as you were lowered
below the frost line.

All those bags – careful
        markings by flower and plant
you put aside for another season.

Passed on to others
        devoted to the soil,
will they sprout – abundant –

erasing the sting of words,
        deeds undone?
Will your green touch

resuscitate unseen,
        healing
a winter of silence?

RAINDROPS
in memory of Ralph Gustafson

Hanging
from the underbelly
of bark,
full
raindrops
wait
for your eyes
to behold them.
They glimmer
for the thousandth
time
not knowing
you have gone
only to return
with words
turning
pages
into your
refined
yet vulnerable
voice.

FROST

Cold
morning,
winter's
reconnaissance
scouts
out
the
terrain
for
a
sortie
of
sudden
snow.

December Flight

These
starlings
swerve
in
flocks,
turning
their
frantic
wings
towards
the
sun's
slanting
light.

VESSELS

As if scattered in celebration
     of God's domestic air,
this show of confetti
     stills the festive
tongue with silent wonder:

foolscap shredding
     sheet after sheet,
       each torn flake flying
then embedding like seed –

today's snow recycling
     feeds into yesterday's
swollen solar pumpkin
     and next season's
blueberry bush
     crowded with vessels
     of pungent wine.

SUSAN ROBERTSON

FAIRY GODMOTHER

Under the weeping tree
where they buried
your mother, she finds you;

separates
the mournful fronds
and finds you;

your back
against the bark,
she finds you.

What should you wear
to the ball?

Cinderella Contemplating the Slipper

This shoe my life, glass;
the knife my sisters used
in vain to win a prince
could not cut deeper.

Sharded glass knows
not false from true.

One misstep
and I rue my sisters' blood
that signalled their deceit.
Better their blood than mine.

Hansel Contemplating His Freedom

Fouler than her leering
breath, the witch's flesh
is burning. My sister
beckons by the door.

I see the path
that led us here
from a woman's greed
to hunger. No more

the witch will dream, but I will.
Behind my eyes, her toothless mouth
kisses the flesh from my bones.
My sister beckons.

I think I hear,
through the stench,
through the fear,
my father calling my name.

The Stepmother Contemplating Snow White

I once had skin
milk could envy, singing
in the pail. My hair,
a flock of ravens.
Two feathers, my lips,
forsaking the breast
of a robin.

Now the pail plucks
its tune for you.
Shall I kill you
or watch you age?

Snow White Contemplating the Apple

Marred by a fresh spot
when I removed it from the drawer
where I store it

so the old men will not see.
I know they would
chastise me.

The spot will grow, the sweet
turn wrong, the flesh
wither: a bright thing wasted.

Every morning the seven beds
to straighten, the seven men
to feed.

I am tired of living here
hidden, surrounded
by small men.

Rapunzel Contemplating Her Locks

He told me tales of love
outside my window
then asked my hair
to bear his weight.

And when he wandered
blinded by the thorns,
tears from my eyes
saved him.

The old woman
envied me my beauty
and locked me up
for none to see.

I shall climb back
to that tall tower,
plait my hair
for none but me.

RUMPLESTILTSKIN'S FANCY
    CONTEMPLATING THE STRAW
for William Wallace

Damn my father.
Damn all men
and their boasting.

Would this king have his treasure
measure my father's folly?
Spin gold from straw?

They may as well ask me
to wring song
from a two day mewling kit,

take my bows,
and make a rhyme
from beaten shit.

FAIRY TALE

When I was six I wanted
to be a princess.

I did not imagine my father
the king, a queen my mother,
no role for a sibling princess.

I did not dream of a distant
prince to save me.
I reigned safe in my turret.

No one could make me
eat peas.

NEXT TO GODLINESS

Cupped hands hold
soap lathered, spread
on arms a second skin,

white and smooth
as a princess.
No wicked witch

as we trace on the other's
back the letters
we are learning:

A for apple the princess
has not yet eaten. B
for her bed in the woods.

Fingers elide the strokes
of childhood, slip
through soap, as the other

strives to recognize
the letter on her skin.

WILD ORCHIDS

I trod through mud
to see pink lady's slippers,

not grown
in any garden.

But in the wood,
the mud-dark wood.

These fairy shoes
do no traveling;

they beckon us.

MUSE

Notice that my head
is wreathed with braids
and my hand lies light
upon my breast.

That my legs are strong
but not slender
and my skin has hidden
from the sun.

That I occupy myself
with pen and paper
but will turn
to watch a heron eat a frog.

A Ball of Twine

He's all man, no bull-
horns adorn his crown,

nor Daedalus construct
his coiled domain.

Yet his mind presides
o'er twisting chambers.

Tie your twine
to something solid

before you enter
this maze.

Rome Did Not Burn Last Night

Rome did not burn last night.
Ilium did not fall.
No hall echoed
the steps of Herakles.

Siren song last night
did not spring
from a sea-grey stone
jutting above lapped waters.

But last night
you turned to hold me,
molding my shoulder
to the curve of your hand.

WHITE BIRD

Not Zeus who turned
into a swan, but Leda.

Her long neck nestling
his chin, stretched

to feel his hand graze
the down of her belly.

And when he touched her there,
he felt her heart

beat beneath white feathers
and kissed her arched neck

all the while a long,
low hiss escaped.

THE SILK ROAD

I robe myself in silk
for you, thin skin
between your flesh
and mine.

So dressed the emperors
and their ladies
when the first worms
were harvested,
cradled for their cocoons
in hidden nurseries.

Birth without fear
of want or prey
cloaked our backs
for centuries.
Now the worms wax white
and moths lie flightless.

Take the silk
from my wanton thighs
and caress my naked skin.

FETCHING

I will wear my mysteries
like silk, a fetch
traveling between
two worlds.

Fetching they say,
something hinted at
in the tilt of the chin, cradled
in the socket of the eye –

thrown out and retrieved,
like a worried stick
in the mouth
of a contented dog.

The Source of the Nile

I think I remember hearing,
or was it reading,
how the Nile began

when some ancient deity
wept tears whose grief
gouged the clay
and filled the channel

that flows from Burundi
past Juba and Luxor
to the Mediterranean Sea.

Your grief so strong, the world
must once have bent
before such sorrow.

VIEW FROM A PLANE

Rivers glowed like Vesuvius
as if crust cracked and wounds
filled with core.

Heavy molten currents
dragged their slag
along smooth banked boundaries,

until the sun no longer
forged the rivers. Water
once more water briefly,

then all below
folded
in the dark.

Nicola Vulpe

WHY MIDDLE MANAGERS NEED POETRY
for Russell Smith, d. 1999

Because there isn't really time

Because we're overworked and overpaid
and can't quite remember anymore
what it is we do

Because we're a favoured consumer profile
but haven't the time

We accumulate airmiles and accessories
some even in real leather

Because we breakfast with strangers
who use our first names

Because we work late

Because we believe in our destiny and our duty
and haven't the time
to reflect or believe or to question

We just make decisions
and live, and die by the consequences

Because we promise ourselves a thousand things

Because we've always wanted to be potters or poets
but stuck with the project to the end

Because we will be better
and are busier

Because we are jealous of greater success
and hate ourselves for not being more clever

We are not indifferent
just not particularly ambitious

Because we drink
and call up past lives and cannot sleep
after they have hung up

Because we make love selfishly
and say we didn't and can't understand
why you say it isn't the same anymore

Because there isn't time

Because we've finally understood
that it doesn't really matter

Tomorrow we'll be fired
– or promoted

Probably we'll be fired

Because we're overworked and overpaid
Because our children could care less
Because there isn't time

Because Russell Smith

is dead

Résumé

Ignore the name,
You'll never say it right.
call me Miles, instead, like the jazzman
and focus, please,
on my accomplishments.

I am Canadian.
I am a nuclear physicist,
B.Sc. from Astrakhan,
Ph.D., Moscow,
12 years beyond the Urals.

I attended many congresses,
was invited to Geneva,
had coffee with Sakharov
and was beaten up for the pleasure.

I speak four languages,
I've published three books of poetry,
all unfortunately in a language
no one cares about anymore.

There were many physicists in my country,
many poets –

I know Microsoft, I know Java,
I understand OOP
and have stayed countless nights till dawn
debugging C++

Focus on my accomplishments.

Call me Miles. Please,
every journey must begin somewhere.

ELEMENTS

We no less than stars
suffer the whims of Einstein's laws

Observe how some end:
a jet of light, a stone hurled
through cold space to earth –

Or linger on, and on,
half-lives halved,
and halved and halved again

Sentimental Poem for Maha

You'll just have to imagine
this is a love poem
just have to look in your own
heart. You know
I'm no good at that sort of thing
no good at love poems

I wrote a few, sure
but that was long ago
was another time
another life, that was…
something that wasn't

And you would want a real one
a real love poem, something
perfumed, polished
intricate as a ghazal
as the tile-work on a Persian mosque
smooth as the inside of an oyster shell

So you'll just have to imagine
that this is a love poem
that it's like a Fairouz song
like her best, for Beirut
only more so

The longing, the nostalgia
unadulterated by music, untouched by voice
by an aging singer,
by violinists sweating through yet another encore
their thoughts already on a nargilé
on a glass of arak

You'll have to imagine the words –
where the words take you
an olive grove, a night among the cypresses
a stone village

You'll have to imagine
the barred courtyard of your school
your grandmother outside

A ripe watermelon
the blue blue Mediterranean –

You know I'm no good at love poems
no good at that sort of thing

THIS YEAR, 2001

In this year, named after a movie
and not yet quite ended,
many things happened

A few hundred species of mollusk went extinct

A submarine sank somewhere off Murmansk,
and while the media and military
agonized over the probability
of nuclear contamination,
300 metres beneath the ice
the crew had a few days
to watch themselves die

In Saudi Arabia and Texas
executions continued as per routine
and the commandment of the Book

Amnesty International published reports

The UN passed resolutions

In Silicon Valley speculators were shocked and
chagrinned,
and executives began layoffs –
these were tough decisions, they said

Cows went mad in England and Scotland and
                                          Wales,
and governments took measures

The Balkans continued being the Balkans

The American president
provoked an incident with China

Palestinians threw stones,
a few brought guests uninvited
to collective suicide events

They were thanked as per routine
with rocket bombs and bulldozers

In Québec many were arrested

A boatload of refugees, shipwrecked then rescued,
was not allowed to land in Australia

An Airbus without engines visited the Azores

Other planes brought the wars home
to Washington and New York

A woman on Rideau Street
lay in the door of a bank
and howled for clean sheets and breakfast

To Moscow, Without Losses

Here it was an item on the morning news

We'd won, the radio said,
the dam had burst, the wall collapsed,
and freedom they said it was,
was flooding east beyond Berlin

So fast it travelled the television crews
were unable to keep up

By the time the first rumours reached us
Budapest had been engulfed
and Bratislava

Icons were defaced, monuments toppled,
but there was little time to fill the streets,
and only moderate rejoicing

East to Warsaw, east to Prague,
east to Tallinn and Kiev,
east to Moscow, without losses,
and the Urals

Workers were caught unawares at tramstops,
children found their teachers in a muddle,

and a pensioner and veteran somewhere
                              unpronounceable
committed suicide

Freedom they said it was

In a matter of hours
it had rippled across ten time zones,
washed through Tashkent,
blue Samarkand and Baikal

Though on account of the time difference
it was not until the next calendar day
that Vladivostok was officially reached

The echo boomed across the Sea of Japan,
and major capitals of the Americas and Europe
                              were annoyed
by a not insignificant increase in smog

Freedom they said it was
though the stock exchanges registered hardly a
                              quiver

Hong Kong and Shanghai were outwardly
                              unaffected,
in Lagos and Bangkok the weather was unbearable,
and the usual number of flights left Mumbai
                              International

In Christchurch the wind was cold for the season,
though on the South Island the sheep,
and the penguins further south still
did not notice

No one was ready for this, said a pundit,
no one prepared

Though strangely,
and perhaps also because television crews
had time to set up

In Sarajevo the effect
was almost immediate

CÓRDOBA

This being Córdoba, you've every right to expect
   the Great Mosque, Maïmonides
   a borrowed lament for the decline of Islam
   and the expulsion of the Jews.

At the very least Lorca
   oranges and olive groves and guitars.

But this being Córdoba,
   I can only tell you how cold it was, how dark
   and how we bluffed our way about the streets
   looking for a place to feed the poet
   and the ambassador.

How we doubled back – twice – and were glad
   they understood less Spanish than they thought.

We lighted at last on a suitable place.

And this being Córdoba they both chose fish:
   the one haddock, the other hake
   and laid back the wine.

The one preferred red, the other rosé
   and demanded the resurrection of tradition.

The first loathed tourists, and had no dessert.

And this being Córdoba there was a Basque girl,
    as foreign as ourselves.

And the walk back was confusing and lonely.

But this being Córdoba
    we made arrangements for their breakfasts
    then saw them to their rooms, the poet
    and the ambassador.

And ourselves to ours.

And this being Córdoba
    in the morning at the AVE
    I bought a paper and a guidebook.

And this being Córdoba
    in the year 900 Abbas ben Farras learned the
                                    secret of glass

And the year following came to grief with his flying
                        machine of feathers and wind
    at the foot of the great tower
    guarding the Guadalquivir.

My Life as a Tourist

In Shiraz, famous for poetry and gardens,
I found a blue tile beside a mosque

But I did not go to Teheran;
the streets there, I was told,
are dusty and sad

Hong Kong was unexpected;
the people are friendly
and the trees very foreign,
but it was difficult to sleep

In Windsor and London I was unemployed,
in Providence I dug graves,
and in Toronto I started on Bay Street

In Richer, at the edge of the prairie,
the water was red and tasted of mud

Montreal was mostly confusing,
Kimiko said: "The best wives are from Kyoto,"
but I did not take up the offer

Valparaíso was all stairs,
and the women were lovely

I did not see Beckett
read a book in the Luxembourg,
but I know he did that once

Did anyone mention the Porte de Pantin,
how at night it looks like a fairground
about to be closed?

I was arrested in Yabello,
in Erbil as well,
but Yabello was worse

In Oulu a granny knitting at the station
sent me to a whorehouse,
when all I wanted was a room

In Muonio I did not speak Swedish

It was 50 below in Karelia,
but the war was over

And at the Finland Station we were fortunate
and shabby enough to melt into the crowd

In Iqaliut I watched the sun roll along the horizon,
and in Awasa I rowed into a rainstorm

From Dhaka to Mombasa
I shivered under the monsoon

But in Dar es Salaam I was able to describe
red dhows and white houses against a green sea

We concluded in Damascus, called Shaam,
with coffee and a fortune teller,
and the day falling into the mountain behind us

I still have my blue tile,
but I have yet not been to Teheran,
sweet Lisbon

Or seen the stars floating
over lonely Dushanbé.

THE AUTHORS

MARK FRUTKIN is the author of six novels and three collections of poetry. His most recent works are *Iron Mountain* (poetry) and *Slow Lightning* (novel), both published in 2001. His novel, *Atmospheres Apollinaire*, was a finalist for the Governor General's Award for Fiction and the Trillium Award in 1988. His work has been published in Canada, the U.S., England, Holland, Spain and India.

As well as writing marketing and advertising copy for a number of high-tech companies, he reviews books for the *Globe and Mail* and Amazon.com. He has taught creative writing at several universities, and attended the Jack Kerouac School of Disembodied Poetics in Boulder, Colorado, where he studied with a number of poets, including Allen Ginsberg and Robert Duncan.

REBECCA LEAVER grew up within sight of Canada, where she now makes her home. She earned a Ph.D. in psychology from the Union Graduate Institute in Cinncinnati, Ohio, and studied depth psychology at the C.G. Jung Institute in Chicago. She has a combined practice in psychotherapy and organization development. Her publications include articles in *The Round Table Review*, a journal of contemporary issues in Jungian psychology, and several professional papers on the presence of archetypes in the workplace.

SEYMOUR MAYNE is the author, editor or translator of more than forty books and monographs. A selection of his biblical poems, *The Song of Moses* (1995), published in Canada and the U.K., was one of the earliest illustrated books to appear in an internet edition. His most recent collections include *Carbon Filter: Poems in Dedication* (1999); *Light Industry* (2000), a volume of humourous and satirical poems; and *Hail* (2002), a selection of word sonnets. He co-edited the award-winning anthologies, *Jerusalem: A Jewish Canadian Anthology* (1996) and *A Rich Garland: Poems for A.M. Klein* (1999).

Over the years he has helped sustain the Ottawa literary community. Founder of the Sandy Hill Gang, he also co-founded the poetry monthly *Bywords*, the poster magazine *Graffito*, and for a number of years he served as MC of the popular poetry reading venue, Bard. At the University of Ottawa he has supervised the publication of a series of sixteen annual anthologies of new writing.

SUSAN ROBERTSON grew up outside Washington, D.C., but now lives in Ottawa. After studying history at the University of Michigan, she worked as a research assistant and technical writer. She did not pursue her interest in poetry until relatively late in her career, when she studied creative writing with Rick Taylor and Seymour Mayne. She was awarded an honourable mention in the League of Canadian

Poets 1999 Canadian Poetry Chapbook Manuscript
Competition, and her poetry has recently been
published in *Vallum* and *Descant*.

NICOLA VULPE was born in Montreal. He studied at
the University of Ottawa and the Sorbonne, where
he earned his doctorate in philosophy. He has
worked as a computer programmer, professional
writer, senior manager in high-tech, and university
professor. Vulpe's publications include a book of
poems, *When the Mongols Return* (1994); a poetry
chapbook, *Epitaph for a Good Canadian* (1998); and
Sealed in Struggle (1995), an anthology of Canadian
poetry about the Spanish Civil War.

ACKNOWLEDGEMENTS

MARK FRUTKIN
Several of these poems were first published in
Descant and *The Fiddlehead*.

SEYMOUR MAYNE
Many of these poems – some in different versions –
were first published in *Arc, Canadian Literature, The
Drunken Boat, The Jerusalem Review, Kerem,
Literary Review of Canada, Parchment, Polynya: A
University of Ottawa Anthology, Trail & Landscape,
Travelterrific, Vallum,* and *Women in Judaism*. In
addition, a number of poems appeared in the
broadsides *Córdoba* (Center for Canadian Studies,
University of La Laguna) and *Five Word Sonnets*
(Sasquatch), and in the chapbook *Hail* (Sandalfon
& Metatron/Concertina).

SUSAN ROBERTSON
Several of these poems were first published in
Descant.

Colophon

The poems were transferred by email; Adobe PageMaker and
Photoshop were the design engines; the text was typeset in
Adobe Minion; and proofing was via Acrobat. Digital from
start to finish.